HAL•LEONARD
INSTRUMENTAL PLAY-ALONG

AUDIO ACCESS INCLUDED

PLAYBACK+
Speed • Pitch • Balance • Loop

 **TENOR SAX**

 FAVORITE Disney SONGS

Audio arrangements by Peter Deneff

To access audio, visit:
www.halleonard.com/mylibrary

Enter Code
3347-6004-3791-5683

Disney characters and artwork © Disney
Disney/Pixar elements © Disney/Pixar

ISBN 978-1-70514-271-4

 **HAL•LEONARD**®

Visit Hal Leonard Online at
www.halleonard.com

Contact us:
Hal Leonard
7777 West Bluemound Road
Milwaukee, WI 53213
Email: info@halleonard.com

In Europe, contact:
Hal Leonard Europe Limited
42 Wigmore Street
Marylebone, London, W1U 2RN
Email: info@halleonardeurope.com

In Australia, contact:
Hal Leonard Australia Pty. Ltd.
4 Lentara Court
Cheltenham, Victoria, 3192 Australia
Email: info@halleonard.com.au

CONTENTS

THE BALLAD OF THE LONESOME COWBOY
from TOY STORY 4

TENOR SAX

Music and Lyrics by
RANDY NEWMAN

EVERMORE
from BEAUTY AND THE BEAST

TENOR SAX

Music by ALAN MENKEN
Lyrics by TIM RICE

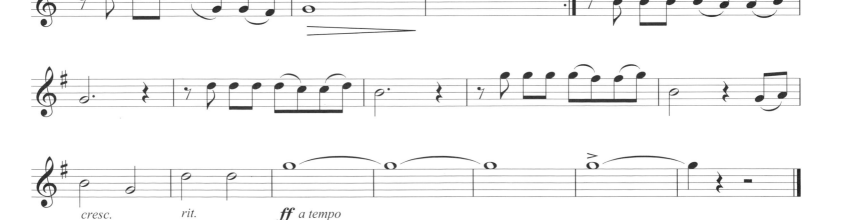

HOW DOES A MOMENT LAST FOREVER

from BEAUTY AND THE BEAST

TENOR SAX

Music by ALAN MENKEN
Lyrics by TIM RICE

HOW FAR I'LL GO

from MOANA

TENOR SAX

Music and Lyrics by
LIN-MANUEL MIRANDA

INTO THE UNKNOWN
from FROZEN 2

TENOR SAX

Music and Lyrics by KRISTEN ANDERSON-LOPEZ
and ROBERT LOPEZ

IT'S ALL RIGHT

featured in SOUL

TENOR SAX

Words and Music by
CURTIS MAYFIELD

LAVA
from LAVA

TENOR SAX

Music and Lyrics by
JAMES FORD MURPHY

LEAD THE WAY
from RAYA AND THE LAST DRAGON

TENOR SAX

Music and Lyrics by
JHENÉ AIKO

THE PLACE WHERE LOST THINGS GO

from MARY POPPINS RETURNS

TENOR SAX

Music by MARC SHAIMAN
Lyrics by SCOTT WITTMAN and MARC SHAIMAN

NEVER TOO LATE
from THE LION KING 2019

TENOR SAX

Music by ELTON JOHN
Lyrics by TIM RICE

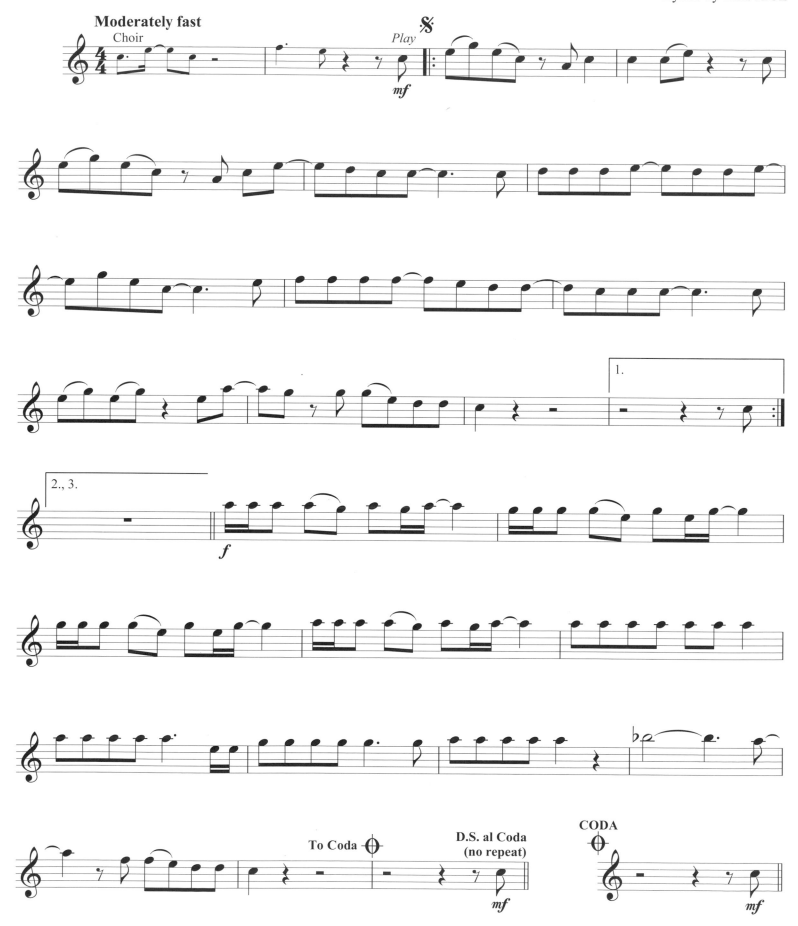

SPEECHLESS
from ALADDIN (2019)

TENOR SAX

Music by ALAN MENKEN
Lyrics by BENJ PASEK
and JUSTIN PAUL

TOUCH THE SKY
from BRAVE

TENOR SAX

Music by ALEXANDER L. MANDEL
Lyrics by ALEXANDER L. MANDEL
and MARK ANDREWS

With spirit
Fiddle and pipe

mf

3

f

Play 4 times

TRY EVERYTHING
from ZOOTOPIA

TENOR SAX

Words and Music by SIA FURLER,
TOR ERIK HERMANSEN and MIKKEL ERIKSEN

YOU'RE WELCOME
from MOANA

TENOR SAX

Music and Lyrics by
LIN-MANUEL MIRANDA

REMEMBER ME
(Ernesto de la Cruz)
from COCO

TENOR SAX

Words and Music by KRISTEN ANDERSON-LOPEZ
and ROBERT LOPEZ